DISCARD

HIP-HOP INSIDER

THE **MEN** OF

HIP-HOP

By Judy Dodge Cummings

CONTENT CONSULTANT

RACHEL RAIMIST, PHD
ASSOCIATE PROFESSOR
DEPARTMENT OF JOURNALISM & CREATIVE MEDIA
UNIVERSITY OF ALABAMA

Essential Library

An Imprint of Abdo Publishing | abdopublishing.com

Published by Abdo Publishing, a division of ABDO, PO Box 398166, Minneapolis, Minnesota 55439. Copyright © 2018 by Abdo Consulting Group, Inc. International copyrights reserved in all countries. No part of this book may be reproduced in any form without written permission from the publisher. Essential Library™ is a trademark and logo of Abdo Publishing.

Printed in the United States of America, North Mankato, Minnesota
042017
092017

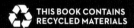

Cover Photo: Robb Cohen/Invision/AP Images
Interior Photos: Larry Busacca/Getty Images Entertainment/Getty Images, 5; Matt Sayles/Invision/AP Images, 9, 70; Evan Agostini/Invision/AP Images, 13; Matt Sayles/AP Images, 15; PYMCA/Universal Images Group/Getty Images, 16, 20; Al Pereira/WireImage/Getty Images, 19; Herb Quick/Alamy, 23; Shutterstock Images, 25, 91; Zuma Press Inc/Alamy, 27, 59; David Howells/Corbis Entertainment/Getty Images, 29; Lee Vincent Grubb/Everynight Images/Alamy, 34; Featureflash Photo Agency/Shutterstock Images, 37; Arnold Turner/Invision/AP Images, 38–39; i4images rm/Alamy, 43; Charles Sykes/Invision/AP Images, 46; Henny Ray Abrams/ AP Images, 49; Greg Allen/Invision/AP Images, 51; Rex Images/AP Images, 54; dapd/AP Images, 57; Steve Black/Alamy, 61; Joe Cavaretta/AP Images, 62–63; Isaac Brekken/iHeartMedia/Getty Images Entertainment/Getty Images, 64–65; Bac To Trong/Daily News/AP Images, 73; Rich Schultz/AP Images, 74–75; Helga Esteb/Shutterstock Images, 77; Jordan Strauss/Invision/Producers Guild//AP Images, 79; Richard Isaac/Rex Features/AP Images, 81; Andrea Raffin/Shutterstock Images, 82–83; MediaPunch/Rex Features/AP Images, 87; Tim Mosenfelder/Getty Images Entertainment/Getty Images, 93; Jeff Kravitz/FilmMagic/Getty Images, 96

Editor: Alyssa Krekelberg
Series Designer: Jake Nordby

Publisher's Cataloging-in-Publication Data
Names: Dodge Cummings, Judy, author.
Title: The men of hip-hop / by Judy Dodge Cummings.
Description: Minneapolis, MN : Abdo Publishing, 2018. | Series: Hip-hop insider | Includes bibliographical references and index.
Identifiers: LCCN 2016962256 | ISBN 9781532110313 (lib. bdg.) | ISBN 9781680788167 (ebook)
Subjects: LCSH: Hip-hop--Juvenile literature. | Rap musicians--Juvenile literature.
Classification: DDC 782--dc23
LC record available at http://lccn.loc.gov/2016962256

CONTENTS

1 HIP-HOP'S RISING **STAR**

A spotlight illuminated the stage in the Staples Center in Los Angeles, California, at the Grammy Awards on February 15, 2016. A chain gang of African-American men led by rapper and songwriter Kendrick Lamar shuffled forward, passing a row of jail cells. Lamar had received 11 Grammy nominations for his hip-hop album *To Pimp a Butterfly*. But before the winners were announced that night, he would perform.

Lamar gripped the microphone between chained hands and stared into the packed stadium. A saxophone wailed and percussion pounded like angry fists as Lamar rapped "The Blacker the Berry," a song both political and personal to the hip-hop artist.

Kendrick Lamar performs "The Blacker the Berry" at the
58th Grammy Awards.

When the song ended, Lamar moved to a second stage, which was decorated as an African village. People dressed in jungle print fabric danced wildly before a bonfire. Lamar sang "Alright," a song that some have christened the new black anthem. Then he stumbled, dreamlike, back to the first stage.

Lamar stood alone, his face twitching with emotion. He delivered his final song, never before heard publicly, in a rapid-fire, aggressive style. When the music ended, an outline map of Africa lit up behind Lamar. One word was stretched across its center: Compton.

PIVOTAL MOMENT

When Lamar was eight, his father took him to the Compton Swap Meet to watch two rap legends, Dr. Dre and Tupac Shakur, shoot a video for the song "California Love." From a perch on his dad's shoulders, Lamar saw Tupac yell at a motorcycle cop for driving too close to his vehicle. In real life, Tupac seemed to behave with as much bravado as he conveyed in his songs. Lamar admired that and wanted to imitate it.

Compton is the Los Angeles neighborhood where Lamar grew up. It is only 14 miles (23 km) from the site of the Grammy Awards, but it might as well be a world away.

Lamar's Journey

Lamar is the oldest child of Kenny and Paula Duckworth. He was born in 1987 and says his childhood was happy, but life was not easy. The Duckworths had three more children after Lamar, and money was tight. The family survived mainly on public assistance.

Gangs were a fact of life in Compton. Lamar's close friends and uncles belonged to gangs, but his love of solitude kept him from following in their footsteps. Lamar also had a passion that kept him off the streets. In seventh grade, Lamar's English teacher introduced him to poetry, and he began to write.

While attending Centennial High School in Compton, Lamar could freestyle rap better than anyone there. When he was 16 he performed for Anthony Tiffith, an executive at a local record label, Top Dawg Entertainment. Tiffith recognized Lamar's talent and decided to represent him. A few years later, Lamar's music got the attention of Dr. Dre, one of the most influential men in the hip-hop music industry. He produced Lamar's 2012 album, *Good Kid, M.A.A.D. City*. The record told the

ODE TO MR. INGE

In seventh grade, Lamar's English teacher, Regis Inge, introduced him to poetry. Lamar had a stutter, especially when he was excited. But poetry became an outlet for his emotions. He said, "You could put all your feelings down on a sheet of paper, and they'd make sense to you."[1] When Lamar performed this poetry as rap, it helped cure him of his stutter.

story of Compton through the lens of Lamar's life. He was nominated for seven Grammys in 2014, including Best New Artist and Best Rap Album. However, the white rap duo of Macklemore & Ryan Lewis beat him in both categories.

Two years and one album later, Lamar was once again at the Staples Center for the Grammy Awards. The Best Rap Album was the highest award Lamar could earn in the hip-hop genre, but he faced steep competition from four other artists, including Dr. Dre himself. The stadium fell silent as the announcer opened the envelope. "And the Grammy goes to," the announcer paused, *"To Pimp a Butterfly*, Kendrick Lamar."[2]

> "He's a singer-songwriter. You can just see the kid's mind like a kaleidoscope over a beat."[4]
>
> —Pharrell Williams about Kendrick Lamar

After thanking God and his family, Lamar gave a shout-out to rappers of the past and made a prediction for the future. "This for hip-hop. . . . We will live forever, believe that."[3]

From Present to Past

Lamar is the latest star in a long line of hip-hop artists who stretch back more than 40 years. In the early 1970s, a new

Kendrick Lamar received a Grammy for Best Rap Album in 2016.

sound echoed through the streets of the South Bronx, a borough of New York City. In basements and city parks, African-American and Puerto Rican youth were creating a unique form of music. There were no bands or singers. Instead, DJs made the music by manipulating records on turntables.

Masters of ceremonies, or MCs, engaged the crowd. They introduced the songs, acknowledged their friends in the audience, and called on the best dancers to show off their moves. Over time, MCs began to dominate the shows as they narrated personal opinions and experiences in fast-talking rhymes and battled each other in duels of improvisation.

When the twenty-first century dawned, hip-hop music evolved again. Some DJs moved from the stage to the music studio. Instead of spinning records by hand, they composed tunes on computers. Rappers were no longer content to just

DJS AND MCS

A DJ, short for *disc jockey*, is a music producer. The earliest DJs physically manipulated records to isolate a section of a song. Today, computer software lets DJs digitally blend any song or sound into a new composition.

MCs are another element of hip-hop culture. They began as DJ assistants. Their job was to excite the crowd with verbal wit. As MCs developed more sophisticated rhymes and showmanship, they became the main attraction for fans.

make music. Some became business tycoons or actors, and their influence on the culture expanded.

Some legendary men of hip-hop excelled at poetic flair, others at bold showmanship. Each man contributed something vital and unique that transformed or enriched hip-hop's sound and style.

HIP-HOP CULTURE

Hip-hop is a set of shared values, beliefs, and behaviors that includes two key elements. The first component of this culture is breaking, or break dancing. Breaking began when DJs began to isolate and extend the instrumental break on a record. Individuals or dance crews battled each other to see who could perform the most physically challenging moves.

Another component of hip-hop culture is graffiti artists. In the 1960s, renegade art appeared on subway trains, overpasses, and the sides of buildings. Writing on public property without permission is illegal, so these artists used code names, or tags, when they spray-painted their signatures on their bold, colorful art.

BEHIND
THE SONG

THE BLACKER THE BERRY

When it was released, Lamar's song "The Blacker the Berry" received more than one million streams in less than 24 hours, but it also sparked controversy.[5] The lyrics explore the struggle of being African American in the United States. Some lines are angry: "I said they treat me like a slave . . . we feel a whole heap of pain, cah' we black." Others are proud: "Black and successful, this black man meant to be special."

In his song, Lamar repeatedly confesses, "I'm the biggest hypocrite of 2015." At the end of the song, he reveals why. Compton gangs are killing each other, so why, Lamar asks, did he weep for the murder of Trayvon Martin, "when gang banging make me kill a nigga blacker than me."[6] Martin was an unarmed black teen who was killed in Florida by a Hispanic man in 2012. Lamar was expressing a controversial issue for African Americans: black-on-black violence in urban America.

The reaction to these lyrics was divided. Some people agreed with Lamar, noting that both police brutality and gang violence damage the soul of African-American communities. But others were critical and argued that by raising the issue of black-on-black violence, Lamar was ignoring the history of racism in the United States.

Lamar received both praise and criticism for his song "The Blacker the Berry."

2 FOUNDING
FATHERS

The music of hip-hop has evolved over four decades, shaped by the creativity of people who appreciate its beats. However, three men stand out as hip-hop's founding fathers because of their technical skills, vision, and an awareness of their audience: DJ Kool Herc, Afrika Bambaataa, and Grandmaster Flash.

Kool Herc—The Beat Breaker

Clive "Kool Herc" Campbell brought DJs, rappers, and dancers together to form the foundation of hip-hop culture. DJ Kool Herc grew up immersed in the vibrant music scene of Jamaica. DJ Kool Herc was exposed to a wide variety of musical genres, from reggae to jazz and gospel to country.

Grandmaster Flash invented hip-hop's quick mix theory.

DJ Kool Herc began building his own record collection as a teenager.

In 1967, DJ Kool Herc's family moved from Jamaica to New York City, New York. It was a culture shock for DJ Kool Herc, who was 12 years old at the time. He left a suburban house with a backyard for a concrete housing project in the Bronx. However, DJ Kool Herc still had music. He sought out and questioned DJs about their craft. He began building his own record collection.

DJ Kool Herc's father was the soundman for a rhythm and blues band. He was responsible for controlling the volume and quality of his band's microphones and amplifiers. DJ Kool Herc's dad purchased a new sound system for the band, complete with massive speakers. However, he could not extract the maximum volume from the speakers. One day when his dad was out, DJ Kool Herc experimented

DANCE BATTLES

Herc's parties allowed gangs to battle on a dance floor instead of on the streets. In the 1970s, dance styles such as the Hustle were popular. This was a choreographed dance with a six-count step, but the Hustle could not keep pace to the new rhythm of hip-hop. When Herc played the instrumental break of a song over and over, the beat of percussion fired up the dancers. They formed a circle and took turns dancing solo in its center. These dancers were not interested in doing the Hustle. They created their own styles by spinning on their heads or popping down into the splits. Herc called these dancers his Break Boys and Girls. This was how breaking began.

with the equipment. By the time his father returned, the apartment's walls were vibrating with the sound of music.

In the summer of 1973, DJ Kool Herc and his sister threw a party at their West Bronx apartment. Approximately 100 teens showed up, and when DJ Kool Herc cranked up the volume of his dad's speakers, the kids went crazy. DJ Kool Herc played funk and soul and used the mic to give shout-outs to friends he recognized. DJ Kool Herc had begun his reputation as a DJ.

Once the parties outgrew the apartment, DJ Kool Herc moved to Cedar Park in the Bronx. When he took breaks, DJ Kool Herc noticed dancers got into the music during the instrumental percussion breaks of a song. However, these sections were usually short.

One night while playing at a club, DJ Kool Herc decided to try to extend these instrumental breaks. He used two turntables and two copies of the record *Apache*. First, he played a drum solo on one record and

DJ Kool Herc continued to deejay in the 2010s.

then quickly dropped the needle on the break of the second record. He repeated this over and over. DJ Kool Herc labeled the technique the merry-go-round and said the crowd was "trippin' off it."[2] This was the start of DJs becoming music creators. This innovation became the heart of hip-hop music.

Afrika Bambaataa— The Culture Maker

Watching DJ Kool Herc spin records inspired Afrika Bambaataa to start a movement that founded hip-hop culture. Bambaataa was a warlord of the Black Spades gang. After several years of bloodshed, the most powerful gangs of the Bronx declared a truce in 1971. This gave Bambaataa an opportunity to redirect his life. He turned to music for inspiration.

Afrika Bambaataa is known for founding the Universal Zulu Nation.

Bambaataa began to DJ at parties. Bambaataa played salsa, rock, soul, and funk, and threw in clips from speeches of Black Power activist Malcolm X. He also formed two rap groups, the Jazzy 5 and Soulsonic Force.

In 1975, when Bambaataa was 18, he traveled to Africa and Europe, where he saw black people living freely and confidently. He returned home with a dream of helping his neighbors improve their quality of life. That summer, Bambaataa traversed African-American and Latino neighborhoods in the Bronx, urging people to join his new group, the Universal Zulu Nation. The organization celebrates African heritage and emphasizes self-improvement. However, Bambaataa was removed as the leader of the Universal Zulu Nation in 2016 after he faced sexual molestation allegations.

The term "hip-hop" was popularized by Bambaataa. As he organized the Zulu Nation, Bambaataa heard some of his rapper friends use the phrase *hip-hop* and thought it

BLACK POWER

The Black Power movement was a radical civil rights group in the 1960s. Activists celebrated African heritage and worked to create African-American political and economic institutions independent from those controlled by whites. Bambaataa admired artists like James Brown, the Godfather of Soul, who sang about African-American pride but did not alienate white audiences. Bambaataa realized music could unify people. This idea led to the foundation of the Zulu Nation.

fit his movement because the music was "hip [cool] and when you feel that music, you gotta hop to it."[3] DJs, MCs, graffiti writers and break dancers came together at Zulu Nation. Their creativity fueled each other.

Grandmaster Flash— The Music Mixer

Hip-hop music is unlike other genres. It is based off of sampling sounds from records and mixing these sounds to create something new. The pioneer of music mixing was Joseph "Grandmaster Flash" Saddler.

Flash was born on Barbados, an island in the Caribbean, but he moved to the United States as a child. He attended DJ Kool Herc's parties and liked the effect of beat breaking, but found it sloppy. Flash decided to find a better way to extend the breaks.

The solution did not come quickly. First, Flash had to locate the right equipment to make his music. He searched through abandoned cars and

ELECTRONICS 101

Flash used to irritate his sisters when he dissected every device in the house, from turntable to toaster, to discover how the machines worked. He could never manage to put the parts back together again properly. Then, his mother sent him to a vocational high school, and Flash learned how electronics worked. It changed his life and music history.

Grandmaster Flash created a new sound for hip-hop.

scrounged through junkyards. Then he went through a lengthy experimentation process. Three years passed before Flash had perfected his quick mix theory.

First, Flash sectioned off his records like a clock, marking where the break of a song began and ended. Then, using two duplicate records on two turntables, he played this break repeatedly. However, unlike Herc's

COWBOY SAVES THE DAY

The first time Flash performed using his quick mix theory, the crowd just stared at him. He realized someone needed to fire them up, but he was too busy spinning records. So his friend Keith Wiggins took the mic and rapped over the beats. Flash said he was like a "ringmaster at the circus."[4] His commanding voice, fast-paced rhymes, and call-and-response style got the crowd grooving to Flash's beats, and Keith "Cowboy" Wiggins, one of hip-hop's great MCs, was born.

method, Flash never lifted the needle; instead, he spun the record. He would cue the break on both records, and then play it on one turntable. When the break ended, Flash pushed in a fader to lower the volume on that turntable and then played the break on the second record. While that break was playing, Flash spun the first record back to the beginning of the break and repeated the process. The beat played seamlessly from one record to the next. Flash was rearranging pieces of music to create a whole new artistic interpretation.

Legacies

DJ Kool Herc never produced a record. In 1977, when he was 22 years old, he was stabbed at a club and nearly died. Herc said the event "killed the juice" in him.[5] He retreated from the music scene and struggled with an addiction to cocaine. However, by the 1990s, Herc was back to deejaying before crowds.

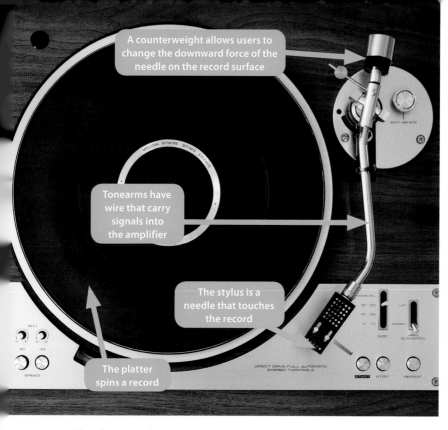

A counterweight allows users to change the downward force of the needle on the record surface

Tonearms have wire that carry signals into the amplifier

The stylus is a needle that touches the record

The platter spins a record

The phonograph was invented in 1877.

In 1982, Afrika Bambaataa's group, Soulsonic Force, released the song "Planet Rock." In this song, Bambaataa created a new sound called electro-boogie rap. The record received international attention, expanding hip-hop culture worldwide.

Grandmaster Flash formed the group the Furious Five, and they released their first album in 1979. Money and fame poured in. In 2007, Grandmaster Flash and the Furious Five became the first rap group to be inducted into the Rock & Roll Hall of Fame.

3 OLD SKOOL ARTISTS

The hip-hop music made between 1979 and the early 1980s was developed for dancing. Raps were simple. Vocal inflections matched the musical beats. This era is known as Old Skool hip-hop. Old Skool artists such as Grandmaster Caz and Kurtis Blow brought the sound of their block parties to radio stations across the United States.

MC and DJ: Grandmaster Caz

Hip-hop fans who aspired to perform faced a decision: Should they be a DJ or an MC? Curtis "Grandmaster Caz" Fisher proved it was possible to do both at the same time and do it well.

Raised in the Bronx, Caz first saw DJ Kool Herc spin records at a party in 1974. The day

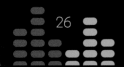

Kurtis Blow was the first rapper to attain national fame.

> **"**I'm basically a battle MC.... I'm here to make you sorry you ever picked up a microphone.... I don't care if God and the 12 disciplines [*sic*] come down here to battle me, I'm busting [them].**"**[2]
>
> —*Grandmaster Caz*

after the party, Caz bought sound equipment and adopted the name Casanova Fly, although later he changed it to Grandmaster Caz.

Caz teamed up with his friend, Disco Wiz, and they set out to make their reputation. Caz wanted to gain popularity slowly and steadily, but Wiz was hungry for fame. So in 1977, the pair decided to have a music battle with the leading DJ of the time: Afrika Bambaataa.

Caz and Wiz arrived at the Police Athletic League in the Bronx with their small sound system. They set up on one side of the gymnasium, while on the other side Bambaataa's crew hauled in massive speakers.

Caz put on "We Will Rock You" by the rock group Queen. The opening beats sounded, but they were quickly interrupted by Bambaataa booming over a microphone, "Caz, we can't hear you."[1] Caz cranked the volume on his speakers up as loud as it could go and started the record again.

Grandmaster Caz gives hip-hop tours in New York City. One stop is the Graffiti Hall of Fame.

royalties from the song, nor was he credited for writing the lyrics. Jackson never publicly denied using Caz's lyrics without credit. Word of the lyrical theft spread through the hip-hop community, and the Sugarhill Gang was booed whenever it played New York City. In 2014, "Rapper's Delight" was inducted into the Rock & Roll Hall of Fame.

In 1979, Caz joined another hip-hop group, the Cold Crush Brothers. They dominated the New York nightclub scene in the late 1970s. The group was famous locally for its high-energy performances. Three MCs would rap at the same time while two DJs worked the turntables. However, Caz was never able to break out nationally and create a hit record.

First of the First

Kurtis Blow was the star of Old Skool hip-hop and the first rapper to achieve national fame. Blow was born Kurtis Walker in Harlem, New York City.

> "I didn't sell a lot of records. . . a lot of people thought my stuff was corny."[7]
>
> —Kurtis Blow on the decline of his DJ career

In 1976, he enrolled at the City College of New York, where he attended classes and became the program director for the college radio station. He worked with a group of party promoters, where he met music producer Russell Simmons.

Blow and Simmons became friends. Both men were looking for a way to break into the music business. In 1977, they opened a club in Queens called Night Fever Disco, and Blow was the house DJ. Simmons convinced him to transition from DJ to rapper and then began managing Blow's career. By 1978, Blow was a city celebrity.

RAPPING THE PULPIT

Following the decline of his rap career, Blow transitioned to a different style of performance. One day while he was reading the Bible, he became so engrossed he couldn't put the book down. Blow became a licensed minister and in 2009 started the Hip-Hop Church. He went on to perform Christian rap with a group called the Trinity.

Through Simmons' management, Blow got a deal with Mercury Records and became the first hip-hop artist signed by a major record label. Blow's single "Christmas Rappin'" was released in 1979 and went to the top of the rhythm and blues charts. Soon after, he released a record with an immediately successful song called "The Breaks." It had classic beats, and Blow rapped out crowd-pleasing call-and-response lines such as, "Throw your hands in the sky."[8]

Kurtis Blow strives to keep all his lyrics family friendly.

This single propelled Blow over yet another milestone. "The Breaks" sold more than 500,000 copies in 1980, making Blow the first hip-hop artist to receive a gold single.[9] However, "The Breaks" would be the peak of Blow's success. Hip-hop music was evolving. Blow's techniques embodied the Old Skool sound with strutting, upbeat party music that had lost popularity with fans. Blow eventually transitioned into producing music rather than performing it.

Old Skool Professors

New York City was full of Old Skool artists in the late 1970s and early 1980s. DJ Disco Wiz was the first Latino DJ. Doug E. Fresh invented beatboxing, a kind of vocal instrument in which he used his mouth, lips, tongue, and voice to produce drum beats and other sounds. Kool Moe Dee of the Treacherous Three delivered tongue-twisting rhymes at warp speed. Melle Mel of the Furious Five rapped the lyrics to "The Message," which was widely recognized as the first socially conscious hip-hop song.

ANOTHER WORLD

Melle Mel decided to be a rapper after he went to Herc's parties. The dances were held in cavernous, dimly lit rooms. Herc's crew of early MCs did not rhyme; they just called out a line now and then. But the sounds echoed around the room. Mel described these dances as psychedelic experiences: "You'd walk in there and you'd be like dumbfounded because it was like you'd just stepped into another world."[10]

But by the early 1980s, fans had graduated from the Old Skool. In 1984, Run-D.M.C. rocketed into mainstream music. With drum machines, raps that echoed, and sleek black outfits, this group presented a polished look with a sharp new sound. The leaders of the Golden Age were poised to take over hip-hop.

4

HIP-HOP'S GOLDEN

AGE

Freedom, experimentation, and individuality are traits that define hip-hop music's Golden Age, from the mid-1980s to the early 1990s. Creative competition drove this era. When a man stepped onstage, he was challenging his peers to top his beats, lyrics, and showmanship. Many artists contributed to the richness of hip-hop music during this period, but three men stand out for their lyricism, leadership, and determination: Rakim, KRS-One, and LL Cool J.

God MC

William Griffin was raised in a musical family in a suburb on Long Island, New York. His mother sang jazz and opera. His aunt was rhythm and blues legend Ruth Brown. As a young teen,

Sean Combs, *left*, LL Cool J, and Queen Latifah take part in a ceremony celebrating LL Cool J's star on the Hollywood Walk of Fame.

Rakim has been called the God MC.

Griffin began writing graffiti and robbing people for money. But during this same time, Griffin interacted with several Muslims in his community. Their words and ideas moved him so much that at age 16, Griffin converted to

Islam. He stopped doing illegal activities and changed his name to Ra King Islam Master Allah, or Rakim for short.

Rakim rapped as a hobby throughout high school and planned to go to college on a football scholarship after graduation. But he also made a tape recording of his raps to take to college with him. Before he went to college, Rakim met DJ Eric "Eric B." Barrier, and his plans changed. Eric B. was convinced the two of them could get a recording deal. Eric B. was roommates with Old Skool DJ Marley Marl, who owned a recording studio. Marl let the pair use his studio to record a demo tape. Marl and his friend MC Shan were present when Eric B. and Rakim made their tape, and they recognized a new type of rapper had arrived. Rakim abandoned his plans for college, and he and Eric B. signed with Russell Simmons's management company.

Rakim and Eric B. released their first single, "Eric B. Is President," in 1986. It became an immediate sensation in the hip-hop community. The duo's first album, *Paid in Full*, was produced in 1987 and received gold status. In 1989, Eric B. and Rakim split up, and Rakim retreated from the music scene. In 1997, he reemerged with his debut solo album, *The 18th Letter*. This record shows the artist

SPEAK UP

When Rakim and Eric B. first recorded their demo tape, DJ Marley Marl and MC Shan did not know what to make of Rakim's rapping technique. His rhymes were complex and he spoke softly. The hip-hop style in New York at the time was loud, with a hard, fast beat. MC Shan yelled out, "More energy, man!"[1] But Rakim did not raise his voice. His poetic lyrics spoke volumes.

grew more philosophical
with age.

Rakim is considered one of
the greatest rappers of all
time. He was the first rapper
to write internal rhymes in
lyrics rather than just rhyming
the last word of a line. Rakim's lyrics are intellectual,
political, and spiritual. His album title *The Seventh Seal* is
a biblical metaphor representing Rakim's opinion that
hip-hop needs to be cleansed of its flaws. Rappers like
Jay Z have called him the God MC, a title Rakim calls "a
blessing."[2]

> "That's what I want to do
> with hip-hop. Tsunami it out,
> hurricane, earthquake and get
> rid of everything that's bad."[3]
>
> —*Rakim explaining the title of
> his album* The Seventh Seal

The Teacher

Another Golden Age artist is Lawrence Kris "KRS-One"
Parker, who has been called both a teacher and a
preacher. He is an artist who both defined and instructed
hip-hop culture.

KRS-One ran away from home when he was 13,
leaving behind a younger brother and sister. He found
refuge in a children's shelter in the Bronx. During the
day he went to the public library and read books on
philosophy and religion. At night he entertained other

kids at the shelter with his raps. For a while, he wrote graffiti under the nickname KRS-One, which stood for Kris Number One. After a brief stint in jail for fleeing the police, KRS-One lived in the Bronx's Franklin Armory Men's Shelter, where he made a friendship that changed his life.

Scott Sterling, a counselor at the shelter, also worked as a DJ on the weekends under the name Scott La Rock. KRS-One and La Rock teamed up to form Boogie Down Productions. In 1987, they released *Criminal Minded*. The album cover featured KRS-One and La Rock armed with handguns, ammo belts, and a grenade. Several tracks on the album were prototypes for the gangsta rap that would eclipse the hip-hop scene in the 1990s. *Criminal Minded* would be their only album together. A few months after the album was released, La Rock was shot to death while trying to break up a fight.

KRS-One carried on, recruiting his brother to DJ in La Rock's place. However, the tone of KRS-One's message had changed. In 1988, KRS-One released *By All Means*

> "Much of what black youth is missing—self-esteem, creative opportunity, outlook, goals—can be traced to what we're not learning in schools."[4]
>
> —KRS-One

Necessary. In this album, KRS-One pioneered socially conscious rap. He addressed poverty, police brutality, racism, and drugs. KRS-One believed hip-hop music was born to move the crowd, but it could also move the mind.

By the early 1990s, fans turned to the new sound of gangsta rap, and KRS-One broadened his focus beyond music. He helped form the nonprofit organization Human Education Against Lies, or H.E.A.L. In addition,

KRS-One was a founder of the hip-hop group Boogie Down Productions.

KRS-One became a regular lecturer on hip-hop history at top universities across the country. His promotion work helped establish hip-hop not only as a music genre but as a culture.

The Lady Lover

Todd Smith, later known as LL Cool J, was a child star of the Golden Age. He rode every wave in hip-hop's journey and remains an icon today.

Smith grew up in his grandparents' house in Queens, New York City. He endured years of abuse. When Smith was four years old, his father shot Smith's mother and grandfather. They both survived, but Smith was traumatized. Later, his mother lived with a man who routinely beat Smith with extension cords, vacuum cleaner attachments, and his fists.

To survive this violence, Smith began rapping when he was nine years old. The music gave him self-worth.

TEMPLE OF HIP HOP

In 1996, KRS-One founded the Temple of Hip Hop. Its mission is to "promote, preserve, and protect Hiphop as a strategy toward Health, Love, Awareness and Wealth."[5] KRS-One spelled hip-hop as one word to demonstrate the unity of the different elements within the culture. The Temple of Hip Hop has become an important organization in preserving hip-hop's customs and values.

When Smith was 11, his grandfather bought him two turntables and a mixer. Soon Smith was making demo tapes and calling himself Ladies Love Cool J, or LL Cool J for short.

SUPERMAN IN A HAT

When LL Cool J was young, he had a daily routine to inspire his confidence. After waking up, he would look into the mirror and slowly put on a hat, adjusting it until it was perfect. Then he would say, "Yeah, now I'm Superman."[7] He did not feel prepared to transition from Todd Smith to LL Cool J without a hat.

LL Cool J sent demo tapes to various record labels and received many rejections. However, everything changed when LL Cool J sent a demo to college student Rick Rubin, who was starting a business managing hip-hop artists. In 1984, 16-year-old LL Cool J signed with Rick Rubin and Russell Simmons's new company, Def Jam Recordings. His first single, "I Need a Beat," sold 100,000 copies.[6]

LL Cool J hit mainstream music with his debut album, Radio, which was released in 1985. LL Cool J's fan base began to grow. His second album in 1987 featured rap's first love ballad, "I Need Love." The song crossed over to the pop charts and reached the top of the rhythm and blues charts. This was a pivotal moment in hip-hop history because, in this era, few rap songs even made the

LL Cool J has hosted many award shows, including the Grammy Awards.

charts. LL Cool J cultivated the image of a heartthrob and broadened hip-hop's fan base to draw in more women.

In an industry where artists peak and fall quickly, this performer adapts to keep his fans coming back. In addition to his music, LL Cool J has starred in movies and television series. He performed during President Bill Clinton's inauguration week in 1993 and has also been a five-time host for the Grammy Awards. Young hip-hop fans today know LL Cool J as an actor and a host, but this Golden Age artist's appeal to both male and female fans was key to bringing hip-hop into the mainstream.

"ACCIDENTAL RACIST"

In 2013, LL Cool J teamed up with country music star Brad Paisley to produce "Accidental Racist." The song is a conversation between a white man wearing a Confederate flag T-shirt and the black man who serves him in a coffee shop. Both men appeal for understanding from the other. The song resulted in a lot of controversy. Some fans felt LL Cool J was minimizing the dangers of white racism. However, the song marked a turning point for country music. It was the first time an artist had addressed the racial symbolism of the Confederate flag.

5 HIP-HOP'S GANGSTAS

The door of hip-hop's Golden Age slammed shut in 1989 when the group N.W.A introduced America to gangsta rap. This music told stories of drugs, sex, and violence with vivid details. Three men personify this era: Dr. Dre, Ice-T, and Tupac Shakur. One for his ability to both create and transform gangsta rap, another for his unapologetic challenge to authority, and the third for his poetic rendition of life on the street.

The Doctor

Andre Young was born in poverty-stricken South Central Los Angeles. When his teenage mother had house parties, toddler Andre manned the turntable. As a teen, Andre preferred going to clubs over running with

Ice-T's song "Cop Killer" received criticism and put him in the national spotlight.

neighborhood gangs. At age 19, he formed a group called World Class Wreckin' Cru and took the stage name Dr. Dre, the Master of Mixology.

In 1986, Dr. Dre met O'Shea "Ice Cube" Jackson. The pair wrote lyrics for Eric "Eazy-E" Wright, a drug-dealer-turned-record-producer who founded Ruthless Records. Ice Cube and Dr. Dre wrote the lyrics to the single "Boyz-n-the-Hood," but the group set to record it refused. The song's lyrics were too explicit. So Dr. Dre, Ice Cube, and Eazy-E formed their own group, Niggaz With Attitude, or N.W.A. MC Ren and DJ Yella later joined the hip-hop group. The group's 1988 breakthrough album, *Straight Outta Compton*, cast Dr. Dre firmly in the public mind as a hard-core gangsta rapper.

> "I was bred for this from birth. My mother has a picture of me in a onesie putting a needle to a turntable."[1]
>
> —Dr. Dre

However, Dr. Dre refused to be pigeonholed as he steered his path through the gangsta rap sensation. N.W.A split up in 1992, and Dr. Dre founded Death Row Records with Marion "Suge" Knight. Dr. Dre's first solo success was *The Chronic*. This 1993 album featured Snoop Dogg, a new artist Dr. Dre was mentoring, and a new sound called

Dr. Dre, *left*, Ice Cube, and MC Ren pose with their awards after N.W.A was inducted into the Rock & Roll Hall of Fame.

G-funk rap. This music had a slow, bluesy beat, and Dr. Dre recorded guitar and bass live in his studio rather than using sampled sounds.

After Death Row Records was established as a major force for hip-hop music on the West Coast, Dr. Dre spent less time on his own music and began mixing songs for other artists. He produced best-selling albums for Snoop Dogg and Tupac Shakur. However, in 1996, Dr. Dre left Death Row after a falling-out with Suge Knight. By this time, Dr. Dre was tired of the stale sound of gangsta rap. He went on to found Aftermath Entertainment in 1996. A few tough years followed. Dr. Dre's new record label performed poorly. Everyone assumed Dr. Dre's career was over, but they were wrong.

GANGSTA DR. DRE

During the peak of his gangsta rap phase, Dr. Dre was living what he was rapping. His mansion in Los Angeles was the site of frequent parties for staff at Death Row Records. People reported deafening music, drunk driving, and living room boxing matches. Dr. Dre also had a criminal record. On different occasions, he was charged with assaulting a police officer, club hostess, and reporter. When he left Death Row Records, he was not just leaving a company; he was abandoning a lifestyle.

Dr. Dre released *2001* in 1999, and it topped the rhythm and blues charts. He also signed Eminem to his label and produced the controversial white rapper's debut album, *The Slim Shady LP*, and its follow-up, *The Marshall Mathers LP*. They both sold millions of copies. Dr. Dre had successfully maneuvered the evolving hip-hop industry and was back on top as a music maker.

In 2015, Dr. Dre released his first album in 16 years. *Compton* was named for his hometown and the subject of the 1989 album he had made with N.W.A. Dr. Dre called the album his "grand finale," signaling, perhaps, that his days as Master of Mixology were over.[2]

"Cop Killer"

Like Dr. Dre, Tracy "Ice-T" Marrow grew up in South Central Los Angeles. He never joined a gang, but he committed plenty of crimes that he says still haunt him. After high school, Ice-T

> "Rap is really funny, man. But if you don't see that it's funny, it will scare the s*** out of you."[3]
>
> —Ice-T

recorded a few singles and starred in some low-budget films. His break came in 1987 when he signed with Sire Records and released his debut album, *Rhyme Pays*, which went gold.

Ice-T's 1991 album, *O.G. Original Gangster*, drew the attention of cultural watchdogs. The record recounted life on the streets of South Central LA with tracks such as "Home of the Bodybag" and "Lifestyles of the Rich and Infamous." However, it was one song from Ice-T's 1992 album, *Body Count*, that catapulted him into the national spotlight. The song was titled "Cop Killer," and it became a turning point in his career.

A police group in Texas threatened to boycott Time Warner, the parent company of Ice-T's record label, because of the song's violent lyrics against law

Ice-T is a popular actor on television's *Law & Order: Special Victims Unit* but still raps.

enforcement. President George H. W. Bush called the music "sick," and 60 US representatives signed a joint letter characterizing the album as "vile and despicable."[4]

Ice-T defended the song as a political statement about the excessive force police exercised over urban youth. He insisted he was not calling on people to kill police but was singing from the point of view of a man who had reached his breaking point.

CENSORED FROM THE START

Ice-T experienced censorship long before he released "Cop Killer." The first songs he recorded were light on violence but heavy on sex. The Parents' Music Resource Center persuaded Ice-T's record label to put a warning sticker on his 1987 *Rhyme Pays* album. A track on his second album, "I'm Your Pusher," also provoked watchdog organizations. Ironically, the song has an antidrug message. In it, Ice-T tries to convince a junkie to give up crack and get high on his music instead.

When Time Warner rejected the provocative artwork for Ice-T's next album, *Home Invasion*, he severed his contract with the company. Another record label produced *Home Invasion*, but its sales were mediocre. Ice-T's popularity with urban African Americans was on the decline. So he transitioned into a successful acting career.

The Poet

Tupac Shakur's reputation for poetic lyrics has only grown since his death at age 25. Tupac was born in 1971 in Harlem to a mother heavily involved in the most radical branch of the Black Power movement. Tupac's mother tried to keep him off the streets. When he was 14, he attended the Baltimore School for the Arts. Immersed in drama and literature, Tupac began writing poetry.

In 1988, Tupac moved to Marin City, California. This was a turning point in his life. His mother had become addicted to drugs, so Tupac took up drug dealing to pay the bills. He also joined the rap group Strictly Dope. Eventually, he got a job as a dancer with the group Digital Underground. Meanwhile, Tupac continued writing his own raps.

In 1991, Tupac released his first solo album, *2pacalypse Now*. One track, "Brenda's Got a Baby," became an underground hit. The song told the story of a 12-year-old

NOT A GANGSTER

After Tupac was imprisoned for sexual abuse, a reporter asked him to respond to allegations that his music was a bad influence on youth. Tupac replied that he was an artist, not a gangster. He said the reason his lyrics were violent was because "Life is not all beautiful, not all fun."[5]

girl who became pregnant by her cousin. She disposed of the infant in a trash heap, turned to prostitution, and was killed. Tupac rapped this tragedy with a heartbreaking matter-of-factness, as if such horror was a daily affair. Two years later, Tupac released *Strictly 4 My NIGGAZ*, an album that featured Ice Cube, Ice-T, and the Digital Underground. This album went platinum.

As a teenager, Tupac Shakur took dance classes, including ballet.

Tupac was a contradictory figure. The sensitivity of his lyrics jarred with the violence of many of his actions. He was charged with several serious crimes. In 1994, he was convicted of sexually abusing a young fan. He received a prison sentence of four and a half years. But after Tupac signed with Death Row Records, its CEO, Suge Knight, posted a $1.4 million bond, and he was released from prison early.[6] Tupac went directly to his studio and wrote music day and night.

Then, on September 7, 1996, Tupac was headed to a charity function in Las Vegas, Nevada. A car pulled up alongside him and opened fire. Six days later, Tupac died. No one has ever been charged with his murder.

Tupac was such a prolific writer that when he died there was a huge backlog of his work. Seven albums and one book of poetry were

THE POWER OF WORDS

The Rose that Grew from Concrete is a collection of 72 Tupac Shakur poems. Thirty-three are love poems. Many have an upbeat, idealist tone. They reference flowers, the dawn, and the green of nature—not the concrete city environment where Tupac lived. These poems were written by the same man who had the words "thug life" tattooed across his stomach. He used this phrase in his raps, too. Tupac used the saying deliberately, not to glamorize crime, but to reach "the kid who really lives the thug life and feels it's hopeless."[7] Tupac knew the power of words in all their forms.

Tupac Shakur's stage name was 2Pac.

released in Tupac's name
posthumously. The themes
of Tupac's lyrics—poverty,
police brutality, failed political
programs, and broken
families—still resonate with
hip-hop fans today.

"I love Shakespeare. He wrote
some of the rawest stories,
man. I mean, look at Romeo
and Juliet. That's some
serious ghetto [expletive]."[8]

—*Tupac Shakur*

6 NEW SOUND AND
STYLE

Men from the East and West Coasts dominated hip-hop music in the genre's first three decades. This changed in the late 1990s.

From New Orleans, Louisiana, came a musical "bounce," a swinging tempo with bass drum samples. Houston, Texas, was the heart of rap with a syrupy drawl. Atlanta, Georgia, rappers told dark tales to a beat with bite. The Midwest refused to conform to a regional sound and instead produced unique acts from one Rust Belt city to another. Outkast, Ludacris, Eminem, and Kanye West stand out at the turn of the twenty-first century for bringing a new sound to hip-hop.

Kanye West infused a new sound into hip-hop.

Antwan Patton and André Benjamin accept their Billboard Music Award in 2003.

Southern Gentlemen

In 1992, Antwan Patton and André Benjamin met at a shopping mall in Atlanta, Georgia. The two 16-year-olds attended the same high school, and after becoming

friends, they held rap battles during the lunch hour. The pair adopted the name Outkast and by 1994 had released its first album, *Southernplayalisticadillacmuzik*. The album's first single, "Player's Ball," went gold, spreading the hip-hop subgenre known as the Dirty South throughout

Ludacris studied music management at Georgia State University.

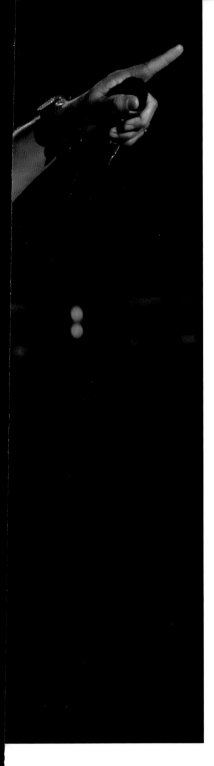

the country. This music had a bouncy beat but not much poetry in the lyrics. Dirty South rappers sang about parties, sex, cars, and money.

The success of Outkast paved the way for another Atlanta star—Ludacris. He gravitated to the forefront of this Southern trend, but quickly demonstrated that his bounce had a deeper side. Ludacris's real name is Christopher Bridges. He was born in Illinois, but he moved to Atlanta when he was 12 years old. During high school, he rap-battled during lunch and made demo tapes after school.

On the strength of one of his demo tapes, an Atlanta radio station hired Bridges as an intern. He created a stage persona: Ludacris. He entertained listeners enough to get his own prime-time radio show, and the producer Timbaland hired Ludacris to work on the single "Fat Rabbit" from Timbaland's 1998 album, *Tim's Bio*.

However, no one offered Ludacris a recording contract. Tired of waiting, he recorded his own album, *Incognegro*. It was released in Atlanta in 2000 and sold 30,000 copies.[1] Recognizing a new talent, Def Jam South signed Ludacris.

RAPPER REFLECTING

Ludacris reflected on his past in a 2015 interview. He was asked if he missed the days when he was young and first found fame. Ludacris fondly recalled the money, clothes, and cars, but insisted, "I'm very happy where I am at right now."[3] As for the future, Ludacris intends to produce music rather than perform it when he reaches middle age because he's "not going to be rapping with a cane."[4]

Incognegro was repackaged and released as *Back for the First Time*. The album showed Ludacris's risqué but humorous side. In the track "What's Your Fantasy," Ludacris raps about sex in an over-the-top way. The album sold more than three million copies.[2]

But Ludacris wanted to be more than the man with outlandish lyrics. *Release Therapy*, his 2006 album, addressed themes of incarceration, child abuse, and the commercialization of rap. Critics and fans praised the album, and Ludacris won two Grammy Awards.

Ludacris transformed his musical success into a movie career that included the *Fast and the Furious* series. Some people assumed his rapping career was over. But in 2015, Ludacris released *Ludaversal* and criticized people who assumed he had given up hip-hop. "I still put music as Number One. Don't you ever forget it," he said.[5]

> "I know I'm the best rapper there is."[7]
>
> —Ludacris

The Real Slim Shady

In 1999, a white rapper burst out of the Midwest with an in-your-face style that took the nation by storm. Marshall "Eminem" Mathers was born in Missouri but spent his teenage years in a mostly African-American neighborhood in Detroit. Although he was not a good student in high school, words always intrigued him. If he heard an interesting word, he wrote it down. Then, he would break the word up into syllables and find words to rhyme with each syllable. Eminem calls this "bend(ing) all the mystic sentence trees."[6]

Eminem started rhyming in Detroit clubs when he was 14. He often won rap battles, but he missed so much school that he failed ninth grade three times. Eventually,

WRITING RAPS

Eminem thought his first rap, written at age 12, sounded as good as LL Cool J's songs. Decades later, he can still recite the rhyme: "Cause before you can blink/I'll have a hundred million rhymes and like a ship you will sink."[9] In an interview, Eminem recalled walking back and forth as he wrote that rap on a small notebook. Today, Eminem still walks back and forth as he composes lyrics. He also writes on paper rather than typing on a laptop.

he dropped out of school to pursue a musical career.

In 1997, Eminem released the *Slim Shady EP*, and it came to the attention of Dr. Dre. He signed Eminem. In 1999, Aftermath Entertainment released *The Slim Shady LP* and introduced Slim Shady to the world. This comic figure, Eminem's alter ego, was featured in the track "My Name Is." The album appealed to both hip-hop and pop fans.

But humor was only one side of Eminem. Some of his lyrics were very dark. In "'97 Bonnie and Clyde," he sings lovingly to his daughter as they drive to the beach. "Oh, where's Mama? She's taking a little nap in the trunk. Oh, that smell? Dada must've runned over a skunk."[8] Women objected to his sexist lyrics, and gay and lesbian groups denounced Eminem as homophobic.

Despite the controversial lyrics, the album sold three million copies and earned Eminem a Grammy for Best Rap Album.[10] In 2000, *The Marshall Mathers LP* set a record for the fastest-selling rap album in history. His music style delivered raps with delirious speed and targeted celebrities and politicians alike with razor-sharp barbs.

With fame came personal failure. Eminem's mother sued him for defamation. He was also charged with assault and sentenced to probation. He became addicted to prescription painkillers.

Throughout these troubles, Eminem continued making music. His fourth album, *The Eminem Show*, was released in 2002 and sold over 10 million copies.[11] He starred in the semi-autobiographical film, *8 Mile*, and a song from its soundtrack, "Lose Yourself," won an Academy Award for Best Original Song in 2003.

UNEXPECTED FRIEND

Openly gay pop star Elton John admired Eminem's music. When Eminem's staff discovered this, they suggested the two perform a duet at the 2001 Grammy Awards to stave off criticism that Eminem was homophobic. Eminem agreed and the two men eventually developed a deep friendship. During Eminem's struggles with drug addiction, John was his sponsor. He called each week to check on Eminem's sobriety.

Eminem released his first solo album, *Infinite*, in 1996.

Eminem's personal demons eventually caught up with him. He almost died from a methadone overdose in 2007, and he finally entered rehab. In 2010, he returned with *Recovery*, an album that exposes his struggles with addiction. Today, Eminem is glad to be sober and wants to keep rapping as long as he has "the spark."[12] But he worries about the day when that spark is extinguished. "Hip-hop is the only thing I was ever good at," he said.[13]

> "There's a difference between me being funny and me being real. I feel like I don't get recognized for my . . . real, true feelings and emotions."[14]
>
> —Eminem

All Things to All People

At the dawn of the new millennium, a DJ-turned-rapper named Kanye West blew out of the Windy City, becoming a hip-hop sensation. West was raised in Chicago, Illinois, in a middle-class home. He received art and music lessons and traveled to China with his mother, a college professor. Despite his privileged background, there was something West wanted that he did not have: a career as a rapper.

West studied music for a year at Chicago State University, but he dropped out to try to break into the music industry. He worked as a telemarketer by day and made music by night. Beat-making is the work of a music producer. He or she uses a computer to compose tunes by programming percussion, instrumentals, or snippets of previously recorded songs into a musical arrangement that is then sold to a rapper. West sometimes stayed up until four in the morning making beats for local groups. As his reputation grew, well-known artists sought out West's talents. His big break came in 2001 when Jay Z, the founder of Roc-A-Fella Records, hired West to produce the beat for his single "This Can't Be Life." West's reputation as a producer was secure and his sound was unique, but he was not content. No one would let him rap.

West did not look like the typical rapper in the early 2000s. He wore pink polo

MIDWEST GRAMMAR

In 2000, the rapper Nelly emerged out of Saint Louis, Missouri, a city rich in musical tradition. Born Cornell Haynes Jr. in 1974, Nelly and some friends formed the rap group St. Lunatics when they were teenagers. Although they produced the single "Gimmie What You Got" in 1996, no recording company offered to sign them. Nelly went solo and was snatched up by Universal Music Group. His debut album, *Country Grammar*, featured the single "Country Grammar (Hot)," which became a hit in the summer of 2000. Nelly's sound was unique. He had a Southern drawl with a Midwest twang. He was one of the first hip-hop artists to sing-rap, and his lyrics are rich with slang and internal rhymes. Nelly's music appealed to both hip-hop and pop fans.

Like West's first album, Nelly's first album was a huge success.

shirts and Italian loafers. He said, "It was a strike against me that I didn't wear baggy jeans and . . . that I . . . never sold drugs."[15] Finally, Jay Z decided to take a risk and let him rap for Roc-A-Fella Records.

The risk paid off. West's debut album, *The College Dropout*, topped the charts in 2004 and earned him three Grammy awards. Both the lyrics and beats intrigued people. It was clear hip-hop fans were hungry for a sound that was not straight from the streets.

Jay Z, *left*, and Kanye West have performed together many times.

Controversy clings to West, but much of it has been of his own making. In 2006, he appeared on the cover of *Rolling Stone* wearing a Jesus-like crown of thorns. He took the stage to protest during the 2006 MTV Europe Music Awards because his *Touch the Sky* music video was not awarded first place. During the 2009 MTV Video Music Awards, when pop and country singer Taylor Swift was being presented with the Best Female Video award, West

bounded onstage, grabbed the mic, and insisted famous pop singer Beyoncé should have won.

West is a firm believer in his talents and has little tolerance for those who disagree. This causes him to be both beloved and condemned. But West is a driven man. One night, West and producer Jon Brion were working late in the studio when West turned to him and said, "I want to be all things to all people."[16] Kanye West is not the only man to have such a goal.

HIP-HOP
TYCOONS

Hip-hop is more than music. It is a culture. Entrepreneurs who recognize this have been able to creatively harness urban African-American culture to create a hip-hop empire.

The Music Mogul

Russell Simmons grew up in Queens, New York City, in a neighborhood riddled with heroin. He dealt drugs for a while before studying sociology at New York's City College. In his spare time, Simmons promoted musical events with his friend Kurtis "Blow" Walker. The success of the song "Rapper's Delight," performed by the hip-hop group the Sugarhill Gang, created a huge demand for rap records, and Simmons

seized the opportunity. He dropped out of college and helped Blow produce "Christmas Rappin'." Then, Simmons formed a management company, Rush Productions, and negotiated a deal for Blow with Mercury Records. "Christmas Rappin'" was released in 1979. Three years later, Simmons began managing his brother's band, Run-D.M.C. Kurtis Blow and Run-D.M.C. became the foundations of Simmons's hip-hop empire.

In the early 1980s, Simmons met a white college student named Rick Rubin at a party. The two quickly realized they each had a talent the other man admired. Rubin was producer for a band called the Beastie Boys and made beats Simmons loved. Rubin valued Simmons's experience because he already managed successful hip-hop artists. In 1984, the two pooled their money and founded Def Jam Recordings, an independent recording company. Their

DIFFERENT MUSIC

Before Def Jam Recordings was founded, Simmons tried to sell one of LL Cool J's singles to a group of white executives from the entertainment company Warner Brothers. Simmons called watching the men listen to the song "a weird scene."[1] They didn't bob their heads or tap their feet. When the song ended, Simmons knew he "didn't belong in that room."[2] Experiences like this one convinced him to form his own recording company.

Russell Simmons, *left*, helped to promote LL Cool J's music.

first single was "I Need a Beat" by a then-unknown teenager named LL Cool J.

Under Simmons and Rubin's leadership, Def Jam grew quickly. It made the careers of many hip-hop musicians, including LL Cool J, Slick Rick, and Public Enemy. Rubin left the company in 1988, but Simmons went on to produce films and founded *Def Comedy Jam*, an uncensored stand-up comedy show that showcased African-American comedians.

" Authenticity sold Def Jam, and honesty. And I think that's what made rap such a stable footprint in culture, that it's so honest. " [3]

—*Russell Simmons*

After establishing companies in the music and television industry, Simmons expanded his business. In 1992, he launched Phat Farm, a men's clothing line. Simmons also created the magazine *OneWorld* and Def Poetry Jam, a televised spoken-word program. In 2001, he helped found the Hip-Hop Summit Action Network, a charitable foundation with a mission to empower African-American communities. In 2016, Simmons produced the All Def Movie Awards. This alternative awards ceremony honors films featuring actors and directors of color. It is hard to say in what direction Simmons will expand his empire next, but he is proud of what he has created so far.

MAKING MONEY

Each year, *Forbes* magazine compiles a list of the five richest rappers. The fifth-richest in 2016 was Canadian rapper Drake. His wealth came from albums, touring, and advertising deals. Rapper and producer Birdman was the fourth-wealthiest rapper. His company, Cash Money Records, produces top performers, including Drake. Jay Z was the third-richest hip-hop artist. His best moneymaker was Tidal, a subscription-based music streaming service. Dr. Dre was second, earning money from the 2015 biographical movie *Straight Outta Compton* and California real estate. Sean Combs topped the list with a net worth of $750 million from his investments in music, clothing, alcohol brands, and media.

All Business

The wealthiest man in the hip-hop industry was a

businessman before he became a rapper. Sean John Combs grew up in Mount Vernon, New York. He watched his mother work multiple jobs to keep food on the table. Combs followed her example. By age 13, he had six paper routes. After high school, he went to Howard University to study business but dropped out to pursue a music career.

Combs interned at Uptown Records in New York City. Within a few months, he worked his way into an executive

Like Combs, Drake is known as one of the wealthiest rappers.

position in charge of recruiting and developing new talent. Combs signed on Mary J. Blige and Heavy D & the Boyz. However, in 1992, Combs was fired due to an internal dispute.

Combs did not let the setback slow him down. He founded Bad Boy Entertainment and ran the company out of his apartment. His goal was to shake up the industry by mixing hip-hop with rhythm and blues. Combs signed Craig Mack and Notorious B.I.G. Their success put Bad Boy Entertainment on a path to financial and musical prosperity by the mid-1990s. Combs also produced music for artists such as Aretha Franklin, Mariah Carey, and Boyz II Men.

However, as Combs's business grew, he also became involved in a series

Sean Combs is both a businessman and a rapper.

of controversies. A feud developed between Bad Boy Entertainment and Death Row Records, the West Coast company headed by Suge Knight. It ended in tragedy when Tupac Shakur of Death Row Records was murdered in 1996 and Notorious B.I.G. was killed soon after. No one was charged for either murder.

Combs retreated for several months but then returned to the music scene with a vengeance. He released his debut rap album, *No Way Out*, in 1997 under the name Puff Daddy. One of its singles, "Can't Nobody Hold Me Down," spent six weeks at number one on *Billboard*'s list of the hottest 100 songs in all genres. The album also won the 1998 Grammy for Best Rap Album. However, one year later, controversy arose again. Combs was charged with assault and illegal possession of a firearm, and he faced several lawsuits. Eventually, the charges and lawsuits were settled, and

KINDER, GENTLER DIDDY

In 2016, Sean Combs decided to reinvent himself again. He wanted to create a "kinder, gentler" self.[4] That softer side became evident when Combs opened the Capital Preparatory Harlem Charter School in New York City in August 2016. The school focuses on preparing disadvantaged students with career and college readiness skills. Combs said this school was "leveling the playing field" so poor urban youth could get a fair shot at success.[5]

Combs decided he needed a fresh start. He adopted the stage name P. Diddy and released a gospel album titled *Thank You.*

Combs has also expanded his business into nonmusical hip-hop ventures. In 2013, he launched a cable venture, Revolt TV. This all-music channel can be accessed on different devices and offers music videos, artist interviews, music news, and performances. He excels at recognizing a consumer desire and filling it. He started Sean John Clothing, created a fragrance line, invested in a vodka company, and produced a television show and several movies.

> "I've always been a businessman first. Even when I pursue my passion in the music industry, I do it from the perspective of an entrepreneur."[6]
>
> —Sean Combs

8 HIP-HOP
ACTIVISTS

Hip-hop musicians have always rapped about issues facing the urban poor. Some speak out only when a crisis arises. Others are identified as socially conscious rappers. Their lyrics wrestle with the tough themes of poverty, war, and societal neglect. In the 2010s, two rappers stand out as men devoted to improving society through their music and community action: Talib Kweli and Immortal Technique.

Son of the Civil Rights Movement

Talib Kweli was born in Brooklyn, New York City, in 1975. His parents, both college professors, told him stories of the civil rights movement of the 1960s. Kweli wasn't the most popular kid in middle school, so he started writing raps in an

Talib Kweli is known as a socially conscious rapper.

effort to be cool. Kweli later said, "Hip-hop . . . gave me a language to speak to my peers."[1]

Friendship fueled Kweli's career as a rapper. In high school, he befriended Dante Smith, a hip-hop artist known today as Mos Def. In 1998, the pair recorded a full-length album titled *Mos Def & Talib Kweli Are Black Star*. The album was praised by *Rolling Stone* magazine for setting a new bar in "conscious, righteous underground hip hop."[2]

Kweli hates the label socially conscious rapper. He believes the title is a way for recording companies to control artists. Although Kweli rejects being labeled, his songs do address social issues. The track "Get By" on his 2002 album *Quality* takes the listener through the struggles some lower-class families must endure. On the same album, the song "The Proud" addresses what Kweli viewed as phony

DOWNPLAYING THE ACTIVIST ROLE

Talib Kweli dislikes the pressure that comes with people identifying him as "some big activist," so he downplays his actions.[3] Kweli argues there is nothing dangerous about "speaking about certain things on record."[4] He insists he is first and foremost an entertainer. If he can do more than that, he will, but Kweli doesn't want people viewing him as an activist, because that takes recognition away from individuals who devote their entire lives to reforming society.

patriotism following the terrorist attacks on the United States on September 11, 2001. His lyrics suggest that fear of a foreign threat made Americans ignore domestic problems. "My heart go out to everybody at Ground Zero. . . . But it's hard for me to walk down the block/Seeing rats and roaches, crack vials and 40 ounce posters," he sings.[5] These were controversial lyrics at a time when patriotism was strong after the September 11 attacks.

> "I want to try to write a song that people can dance to. But how can I focus on that when there's so much other suffering?"[7]
>
> —Talib Kweli

Kweli stands out from other activist rappers because of his willingness to take action off the stage. When a group of young activists named the Dream Defenders occupied the Florida statehouse in 2013, Kweli showed up to support them. The Dream Defenders demanded the governor support a bill to address racial profiling after the acquittal of George Zimmerman, the man who shot and killed 17-year-old Trayvon Martin. In 2012, Martin was visiting his father in Sanford, Florida. Zimmerman saw Martin in the neighborhood and called the police to report him as "a suspicious person."[6] Zimmerman confronted Martin and ended up shooting and killing him.

HIP-HOP
ACTIVISM

There are benefits and risks to being an activist rapper, something Macklemore and Ryan Lewis know from experience.

Ben "Macklemore" Haggerty and producer Ryan Lewis are the most well-known white rappers since Eminem. The duo performed its song about marriage equality, "Same Love," at the 2014 Grammy Awards. During the song, 33 couples, some gay and some straight, came forward and were married before a televised audience. There was some backlash from the public, but overall, "Same Love" was welcomed by fans.

The same is not true for "White Privilege II," a track on the duo's 2016 album, *This Unruly Mess I've Made*. The song explores Macklemore's feelings about whether he had the right to march with African-American protesters following the police killing of an unarmed African-American teen. Macklemore rapped, "I want to take a stance cause we are not free / And then I thought about it, we are not 'we.'"[8]

Some African Americans have expressed frustration with this song. They say that, as a white man, Macklemore is praised for rapping about his emotional struggles, while African-American rappers are criticized for expressing theirs. Macklemore accepted the criticism and intends to carry on making music that matters.

Macklemore has written songs that address controversial topics within the United States.

When Kweli was asked why he was there, he said, "When you have a voice and a platform . . . it becomes your moral obligation to support that community."[9] Excessive use of force by police, sexist and homophobic lyrics in rap music, and the growing income inequality in America are causes that have drawn Kweli to the streets to protest and to his notebook to write lyrics.

REVOLUTIONARIES

During his year in prison, Immortal Technique studied the works of Malcolm X and Che Guevara. Malcolm X was an African-American civil rights activist and Muslim leader. In the 1950s and 1960s, Malcolm X challenged the ideals of the civil rights movement promoted by Martin Luther King Jr. Unlike King's call for peaceful, nonviolent protests, Malcolm X encouraged followers to defend themselves against white aggression.

Che Guevara is known for his role in working with Fidel Castro to overthrow the Cuban government during the Cuban Revolution in the late 1950s. After its success, Guevara became the president of the National Bank of Cuba and traveled the world. He encouraged revolutions in developing countries.

Child of the Third World

With spitfire intensity, rapper Immortal Technique demands that his listeners wake up to the struggles of the global poor. Immortal Technique's name is Felipe Coronel. He was born in Lima, Peru, and his family moved to Harlem when he was two years old. He began rapping seriously as a teenager. While attending Pennsylvania State University, Coronel

Immortal Technique has traveled across the globe to perform his music.

PRIVATE FAITH

Immortal Technique has lyrics about religion, but he refuses to name his faith. The rapper is convinced if he publicly identified as Christian, Jewish, or Muslim, his lyrics would be scrutinized for religious bias rather than considered for deeper truths. Besides, the artist says, "I believe in God and . . . that faith is between me and God."[11]

was arrested for assault and spent a year in prison. While incarcerated, he read the work of revolutionaries Che Guevara and Malcolm X, and he wrote songs. Upon release, Coronel returned to Harlem, where he worked odd jobs by day and battled other rappers by night. His skills grew, along with his reputation.

In 2001, Coronel, known by then as Immortal Technique, released his debut album, *Revolutionary Vol. 1*. He formed his own record label, Viper, so he could control his art. His 2008 album, *The 3rd World*, demonstrates the global scope of the issues that concern him. The title track takes listeners to areas of the world most American rappers don't address: "I'm from where the gold and diamonds are ripped from the earth / Right next to the slave castles where the water is cursed."[10] The lyrics are as raw and violent as any gangsta rap song, but they address global inequalities.

In addition, Immortal Technique makes comparisons between the struggle for survival in the Third World and life on the streets of the Bronx or Los Angeles. He once told a reporter, "I'm not a positive rapper. I rhyme about rape, murder, torture, about the 'hood and drugs. . . . I relate it to the Third World."[12] He calls his music Reality Rap and insists music fans deserve and desire this complex and controversial material. Immortal Technique believes people care deeply about global problems, but they need someone to present information about these issues in a relatable way. He argues that no one needs a college degree to understand the messages behind his lyrics.

"If you're troubled by the words I speak, then you should probably hang yourself because the world is going to tear you apart or is too real for you to accept."[13]

—*Immortal Technique*

Immortal Technique has seen what he raps about. In 2009, his music tours took him to war-torn Afghanistan. In Haiti, he saw a 10-year-old girl caring for orphaned toddlers. In Peru, he witnessed a preteen prostituting herself to survive. These tragedies compel him to create music.

Kendrick Lamar performs his song "Alright" at the 2016 Grammy Awards.

While the stage is where Immortal Technique's activism speaks loudest, he also acts directly to help improve peoples' lives. In 2009, he partnered with a nonprofit organization in Afghanistan to build an orphanage, clinic, and school in the city of Kabul. This rapper is moved by what he calls "righteous fury."[14] He is convinced he will continue to make music in some capacity forever. Because, in his words, "There is much work left to do."[15]

Social consciousness is now at the forefront of hip-hop music. New artists such as Kendrick Lamar and established veterans such as Jay Z are boldly challenging fans to take a stand on issues they care about. Hip-hop artists rap about what they see on the streets of the United States and internationally. Whether fans will heed the messages of this music is a story that must be told by the rappers of the future.

TIMELINE

1973

DJ Kool Herc plays music for a party in his apartment complex. Some hip-hop historians consider this event the birth of hip-hop culture.

1975

Afrika Bambaataa forms the Universal Zulu Nation.

1979

"Rapper's Delight" is released. It is the first commercially produced rap record.

1980

The song "The Breaks" sells more than 500,000 copies, making Kurtis Blow the first hip-hop artist to make a gold single.

1984

Russell Simmons and Rick Rubin found Def Jam Recordings.

1987

LL Cool J releases "I Need Love," rap's first love song.

1988

In August, N.W.A releases *Straight Outta Compton*, one of the original gangsta rap albums; KRS-One releases *By All Means Necessary*, an early socially conscious album.

1992

Ice-T releases the album *Body Count* and receives national criticism for the lyrics to "Cop Killer."

1996

In September, Tupac Shakur is shot to death.

1997

Rakim releases his solo debut, *The 18th Letter*.

2000

In May, Eminem releases *The Marshall Mathers LP*. It becomes the fastest-selling rap record in history.

2004

Kanye West earns three Grammys for *The College Dropout*, the first record on which he demonstrated his skills as a rapper.

2006

Ludacris wins a Grammy Award for Best Rap Album for *Release Therapy*.

2007

Grandmaster Flash and the Furious Five becomes the first hip-hop group to be inducted into the Rock & Roll Hall of Fame.

2009

Immortal Technique travels to Afghanistan as part of his partnership with a nonprofit organization to construct an orphanage, clinic, and school for war orphans.

2013

In August, Talib Kweli joins a sit-in movement in Florida to protest racial bias in state laws.

2016

In February, Kendrick Lamar wins a Grammy for Best Rap Album for *To Pimp a Butterfly*.

ESSENTIAL
FACTS

KEY PLAYERS

- DJ Kool Herc was the first to figure out how to play extended breaks on records.

- DJ Grandmaster Flash was the first to mix records using two turntables and a mixer.

- Afrika Bambaataa founded the Zulu Nation in 1975 and decided to use music to improve his community. He brought DJs, dancers, graffiti writers, and MCs together. The Zulu Nation's motto was Peace, Love, Unity and Having Fun.

- Kurtis Blow was the first rapper to be represented by a major record label and to have a gold single.

- KRS-One is considered to be a teacher and a preacher. He was one of the first socially conscious rappers.

- LL Cool J is a rapper whose songs crossed over into the pop music genre.

- Tupac Shakur is known for his poetic lyrics.

- Kanye West is a producer and rapper from Chicago. He proved a hip-hop artist could be successful without having come up from life on the streets.

- Talib Kweli raps about political and social issues confronting African Americans and participates in civil rights protests.

TRENDS

- In the 1970s, key elements of hip-hop culture were founded by DJ Kool Herc, Afrika Bambaataa, and Grandmaster Flash.

- Old Skool hip-hop dominated the New York music scene in the mid-1970s. This was mostly party music with a good dancing beat that was performed live.

- The Golden Age of hip-hop lasted from the late 1970s to the early 1980s. It was characterized by a wide variety of styles and sounds as artists experimented. At this time, more hip-hop music was recorded and distributed across the nation.

- In the 1990s, the subgenre known as gangsta rap dominated hip-hop music. Artists from the West Coast introduced stories of street life into their lyrics.

- In the early 2000s, the popularity of gangsta rap declined, and artists from the South and Midwest introduced new sounds and styles.

- In the second decade of the twenty-first century, artists began producing music with political and social messages, particularly related to civil rights issues facing African Americans.

LEGACY

Hip-hop artists use their life experiences to tell stories through songs that are designed to entertain, educate, and inspire their audiences. In doing so, these artists continue to transform the sound and style of hip-hop culture.

QUOTE

"To me, hip hop says, 'Come as you are.' . . . It ain't about bling-bling. . . . It is not about me being better than you or you being better than me. It's about you and me, connecting one to one."

—*DJ Kool Herc*

GLOSSARY

BLACK POWER

A movement led by African Americans in the 1960s to gain political and economic equality.

BREAK

The instrumental section of a song, usually identified with a percussion solo.

CENSORSHIP

The act of imposing values on others by limiting what they may read, write, hear, or see.

FADER

A device for varying the volume on an audio player.

GANGSTA RAP

A type of rap music with lyrics featuring the violence and drug use of urban gang life.

GENRE

A specific type of music, film, or writing.

HOMOPHOBIC

Fearing or feeling hostility toward gay people.

JAZZ

A genre of music developed by African Americans in New Orleans in the early 1900s.

MIXER

An audio machine used by DJs to make smooth transitions between recorded sounds as they are being played.

PRODUCER

The person who supervises the sampling, mixing, and recording of music and also guides the performers.

RACISM

Inferior treatment of a person or group of people based on race.

REGGAE

A genre of music that originated in Jamaica.

ROYALTIES

A share of money generated by sales of a work.

SAMPLE

A piece of recorded music used by DJs or producers to make new music.

ADDITIONAL RESOURCES

SELECTED BIBLIOGRAPHY

Bynoe, Yvonne. *Encyclopedia of Rap and Hip-Hop Culture*. Westport, CT: Greenwood, 2006. Print.

Chang, Jeff. *Can't Stop Won't Stop: A History of the Hip-Hop Generation*. New York: St. Martin's, 2005. Print.

Price, Emmett G., III. *Hip Hop Culture*. Santa Barbara, CA: ABC-CLIO, 2006. Print.

Watkins, S. Craig. *Hip Hop Matters: Politics, Pop Culture, and the Struggle for the Soul of a Movement*. Boston, MA: Beacon, 2005. Print.

FURTHER READINGS

Bua, Justin. *The Legends of Hip Hop*. New York: Harper Design, 2011. Print.

Piskor, Ed. *Hip Hop Family Tree*. Seattle, WA: Fantagraphics Books, 2014. Print.

WEBSITES

To learn more about Hip-Hop Insider, visit **abdobooklinks.com**. These links are routinely monitored and updated to provide the most current information available.

FOR MORE INFORMATION

For more information on this subject, contact or visit the following organizations:

HARLEM HIP HOP TOURS
69 W. 106th Street, Suite 5B
New York, NY 10025
800-655-2091
http://harlemhiphoptours.com/
This private company offers a live DJ bus tour of key sites in hip-hop history that are located in New York City.

ROCK & ROLL HALL OF FAME
1100 Rock and Roll Boulevard,
Cleveland, OH 44114
216-781-7625
www.rockhall.com
Although most of this museum is devoted to rock musicians, there are several hip-hop artists represented, and more are being considered for induction each year.

SMITHSONIAN MUSEUM OF AFRICAN AMERICAN HISTORY AND CULTURE
1400 Constitution Avenue NW
Washington, DC 20560
1-844-750-3012
https://nmaahc.si.edu/
This museum has an exhibit titled "Musical Crossroads." It traces the evolution of black music from the time Africans first arrived in America up to the present, including the evolution of hip-hop.

SOURCE NOTES

CHAPTER 1. HIP-HOP'S RISING STAR

1. Josh Eels. "The Trials of Kendrick Lamar." *Rolling Stone.* Rolling Stone, 22 June 2015. Web. 1 Mar. 2017.

2. Recording Academy/Grammys. "Kendrick Lamar Best Rap Album." *YouTube.* YouTube, 15 Feb. 2016. Web. 28 Feb. 2017.

3. Lizzy Goodman. "Kendrick Lamar, Hip-Hop's Newest Old-School Star." *New York Times Magazine.* The New York Times, 25 June 2014. Web. 28 Feb. 2017.

4. Ibid.

5. Spencer Kornhaber. "Kendrick Lamar is not a Hypocrite." *The Atlantic.* Atlantic Monthly Group, 11 Apr. 2015. Web. 9 Oct. 2016.

6. Ibid.

CHAPTER 2. FOUNDING FATHERS

1. Jeff Chang. *Can't Stop Won't Stop: A History of the Hip-Hop Generation.* New York: St. Martin's, 2005. Print.

2. Angus Batey. "DJ Kool Herc DJs His First Block Party (His Sister's Birthday) at 1520 Sedgwick Avenue, Bronx, New York." *Guardian.* Guardian News and Media Limited, 12 June 2011. Web. 28 Feb. 2017.

3. CornellSunVideo. "Afrika Bambaataa Talks about the Roots of Hip Hop." *YouTube.* YouTube, 27 Nov. 2012. Web. 10 Oct. 2016.

4. "DJ and Hip-Hop Pioneer Grandmaster Flash." *Fresh Air.* NPR, 29 Aug. 2005. Web. 4 Nov. 2016.

5. Davey D. "Interview w/ DJ Kool Herc." *Hip Hop History 101.* Davey D, n.d. Web. 2 Nov. 2016.

CHAPTER 3. OLD SKOOL ARTISTS

1. Cornell University Library. "A Conversation with Hip Hop's Pioneers." *Cornell Cast.* Cornell University, 12 Feb. 2009. Web. 28 Feb. 2017.

2. Ibid.

3. Ibid.

4. Ibid.

5. Sarah Thompson. "The Secret Ghostwriters of Hip Hop." *BBC News.* BBC. 6 Aug. 2014. Web. 5 Nov. 2016.

6. Cornell University Library. "A Conversation with Hip Hop's Pioneers." *Cornell Cast.* Cornell University, 12 Feb. 2009. Web. 28 Feb. 2017.

7. Kurtis Blow. "The Breaks." *Google Play Music.* Google, n.d. Web. 28 Feb. 2017.

8. "Blow, Kurtis." *Encyclopedia.com.* Encyclopedia.com, n.d. Web. 5 Nov. 2016.

9. Emmett G. Price, III. *Hip Hop Culture.* Santa Barbara, CA: ABC-CLIO, 2006. Print. 13.

10. "Rapper Melle Mel: Delivering 'The Message.'" *Fresh Air.* NPR, 29 Aug. 2005. Web. 5 Nov. 2016.

CHAPTER 4. HIP-HOP'S GOLDEN AGE

1. Jeff Chang. *Can't Stop Won't Stop: A History of the Hip-Hop Generation.* New York: St. Martin's, 2005. Print. 257.

2. "Rakim: The MC Reveals His 'Seventh Seal.'" *All Things Considered.* NPR, 21 Nov. 2009. Web. 6 Nov. 2016.

3. Ibid.

4. Craig S. Watkins. *Hip Hop Matters: Politics, Pop Culture, and the Struggle for the Soul of a Movement.* Boston, MA: Beacon, 2005. Print. 241.

5. Ibid. 242.

6. Yvonne Bynoe. *Encyclopedia of Rap and Hip Hop Culture.* Westport, CT: Greenwood, 2006. Print. 226–227.

7. LL Cool J. *I Make My Own Rules.* New York: St. Martin's, 1997. Print. 80.

CHAPTER 5. HIP-HOP'S GANGSTAS

1. Cal Fussman. "Dr. Dre: What I've Learned." *Esquire.* Hearst Communications, 11 Dec. 2013. Web. 28 Feb. 2017.

2. Timmhotep Aku. "After 16 Years, Dr. Dre Returns With 'Compton.'" *NPR Music.* NPR, 7 Aug. 2015. Web. 28 Feb. 2017.

3. Alan Light. "The Rolling Stone Interview: Ice-T." *Rolling Stone.* Rolling Stone, 20 Aug. 1992. Web. 28 Feb. 2017.

4. Ibid.

5. Chuck Philips. "Tupac Shakur: 'I Am Not a Gangster.'" *Los Angeles Times.* Los Angeles Times, 25 Oct. 1995. Web. 28 Feb. 2017.

6. "Dr. Dre VIBE Cover Story 'Life From Death Row.'" *Vibe.* Vibe, 16 Dec. 2012. Web. 28 Feb. 2017.

7. YouTube. "Tupac Interview about Definition of Thug Life." *YouTube.* YouTube, n.d. Web. 28 Feb. 2017.

8. Chuck Philips. "Tupac Shakur: 'I Am Not a Gangster.'" *Los Angeles Times.* Los Angeles Times, 25 Oct. 1995. Web. 28 Feb. 2017.

CHAPTER 6. NEW SOUND AND STYLE

1. "Ludacris." *Encyclopedia.* Encyclopedia.com, n.d. Web. 28 Feb. 2017.

2. Ibid.

3. Simon Vozick-Levinson. "Ludacris on 'Ludaversal': 'This Sh-- Is Out of Control.'" *Rolling Stone.* Rolling Stone, 10 Apr. 2015. Web. 28 Feb. 2017.

4. Ibid.

5. Ibid.

6. "Eminem: American Musician." *Encyclopedia Britannica.* Encyclopedia Britannica, 6 Mar. 2016. Web. 28 Feb. 2017.

7. Simon Vozick-Levinson. "Ludacris on 'Ludaversal': 'This Sh-- Is Out of Control.'" *Rolling Stone.* Rolling Stone, 10 Apr. 2015. Web. 28 Feb. 2017.

SOURCE NOTES
CONTINUED

8. "'97 Bonnie and Clyde." Genius.com. Genius Media Group, n.d. Web. 9 Nov. 2016.

9. Josh Eells. "Eminem: On the Road Back From Hell" *Rolling Stone*. Rolling Stone, 17 Oct. 2011. Web. 28 Feb. 2017.

10. "Eminem Bio." *Rolling Stone*. Rolling Stone, n.d. Web. 28 Feb. 2017.

11. Ibid.

12. Josh Eells. "Eminem: On the Road Back From Hell" *Rolling Stone*. Rolling Stone, 17 Oct. 2011. Web. 28 Feb. 2017.

13. Ibid.

14. Anthony Bozza. "Eminem." *Rolling Stone*. Rolling Stone, 21 Jan. 2015. Web. 28 Feb. 2017.

15. Josh Tyrangiel. "Why You Can't Ignore Kanye." *Time* 166.9 (2005): 54-61. *Academic Search Premier*. Web. 8 Oct. 2016.

16. Ibid.

CHAPTER 7. HIP-HOP TYCOONS

1. "Rick Rubin, Russell Simmons: Def Jam's First 25 Years." *NPR Music*. NPR, 9 Oct. 2011. Web. 28 Feb. 2017.

2. Ibid.

3. Ibid.

4. Christopher R. Weingarten. "Inside Bad Boy Family Reunion, 2016's Most Hit-Packed Tour." *Rolling Stone*. Rolling Stone, 13 Sept. 2016. Web. 28 Feb. 2017.

5. "Hip Hop Mogul Sean 'Diddy' Combs on His Move From 'Me' to 'We.'" *CBS News*. CBS Interactive, 29 Sept. 2016. Web. 28 Feb. 2017.

6. Roberto A. Ferdman. "Music Made Sean 'Diddy' Combs Famous, but Here's What Made Him Rich." *Washington Post*. Washington Post, 2 Oct. 2015. Web. 28 Feb. 2017.

CHAPTER 8. HIP-HOP ACTIVISTS

1. "Talib Kweli Biography." *Musician Guide*. Net Industries, n.d. Web. 28 Feb. 2017.

2. Ibid.

3. Jeff Chang. "An Uplifting Voice Of Hip-Hop." *Progressive* 69.10 (2005): 42-44. Academic Search Premier. Web. 9 Oct. 2016.

4. Ibid.

5. "Proud." *Genius.com*. Genius Media Group, n.d. Web. 28 Feb. 2017.

6. "Trayvon Martin Shooting Fast Facts." *CNN*. Cable News Network, 28 Feb. 2017. Web. 28 Feb. 2017.

7. Jeff Chang. "An Uplifting Voice Of Hip-Hop." *Progressive* 69.10 (2005): 42-44. Academic Search Premier. Web. 28 Feb. 2017.

8. "White Privilege II." *Genius.com*. Genius Media Group, n.d. Web. 28 Feb. 2017.

9. AJ Vicens. "Talib Kweli Stands His Ground." *Mother Jones*. Mother Jones and the Foundation for National Progress, 26 Aug. 2013. Web. 28 Feb. 2017.

10. "The 3rd World." *Genius.com.* Genius Media Group, n.d. Web. 28 Feb. 2017.

11. Omar Shahid. "Immortal Technique: 'I'm Seen as a Threat to the Status Quo of Hip-Hop.'" *Guardian.* Guardian News and Media Limited, 25 Oct. 2012. Web. 28 Feb. 2017.

12. "Immortal Technique: Rock The Boat (Part II)." *XXL.* XXL Network, 5 Apr. 2006. Web. 28 Feb. 2017.

13. Omar Shahid. "Immortal Technique: 'I'm Seen as a Threat to the Status Quo of Hip-Hop.'" *Guardian.* Guardian News and Media Limited, 25 Oct. 2012. Web. 28 Feb. 2017.

14. Ibid.

15. Raquel Cepeda. "More Articulate, Politically Charged Flame-Throwing from Immortal Technique." *Village Voice.* Village Voice, 29 July 2016. Web. 28 Feb. 2017.

INDEX

ABOUT THE AUTHOR

Judy Dodge Cummings is a writer and former history teacher from Wisconsin. She has written numerous nonfiction books for children and teenagers. Her other title about hip-hop music is *Macklemore & Ryan Lewis: Grammy-Winning Hip-Hop Duo.*